GREETINGS FROM CAMP WEFOWASA

Jay W. Foreman

Mark Sasser

Publishing Made Easy

ISBN: 979-8-9854044-5-6 (Paperback)
ISBN: 979-8-9854044-4-9 (eBook)

This story is dedicated to four of my favorite campers:

Robert E. Aylor III

Dale “Wimp” Barley

Earl Foreman

Bob Wells

Greetings from Camp Wefowasa

School was almost over and that meant just one thing for Leonard...Summer Camp! It was his favorite time of the year. He was excited to decide which camp he would attend. Barry Patch, the Head Counselor from Camp Wefowasa was visiting his school, handing out brochures. Leonard took one and started reading.

Come
Camp
US!

Welcome to Camp Wefowasa! This Summer, let us spoil you with our Five-Star accommodations. They are Five-Star because that’s how many stars you’ll see through the holes in our tents.

Speaking of holes, our canoes allow campers to enjoy boating *and* swimming at the same time!

Worried about missing your pets? We have plenty of wildlife to help take your mind off them! And if you don’t have time to find them, no problem. They’ll find you.

Do you enjoy delicious meals? Of course, you do! And you'll enjoy them even more after eating what we serve you during your time with us!

REGULATIONS
VAL

Be prepared to make lifelong friends.
Some may never want to let you go!

Ever wonder just how itchy poison ivy can be? Stop wondering and come find out during one of our nature hikes!

CAMP

Enjoy receiving letters from your family. Les Efficient, our Postmaster General, is ninety-six years young and still won’t retire. Sometimes he gets confused and mixes up mail, but that’s okay. The care package you get might not be meant for you, but it may be something better!

LES

Ever since our athletic budget was slashed, we have had to share equipment among our different sports. And you'll love it! Do you know how hard it is to strike out when swinging at a basketball?

Do you enjoy arts and crafts? Use your imagination to come up with new and exciting ways to use popsicle sticks! Seriously, it's completely up to you. Our Arts & Crafts Counselor quit last month so you can do anything you want!

Come and experience our weekly bonfires! Sing camp songs. Tell scary stories. Act in funny skits. This Summer, we will have an extra fire extinguisher on hand. We learned our lesson from last year. On another note, our Fire Marshall, Bernie Woods, says most of his eyebrows have grown back since last year's *incident*.

Leonard handed the brochure back to Barry. “I’m confused. It seems like things aren’t that great at Camp Wefowasa, but you make it sound like they are.”

Barry smiled and replied, “The way things are at Camp Wefowasa is completely up to you.”

“I don’t understand,” said Leonard.

“The choice is yours,” Barry explained. “You’re going to have this choice to make in everything you do for the rest of your life. You can choose to see the good in each situation or the bad. Whichever you look for, I promise you’ll find.”

Leonard learned an important lesson that day. There will always be good and bad in the world. Whenever we choose to focus on the good, not only will we find it, we will help make a good situation great.

Leonard went to Camp Wefowasa that Summer and had the best time of his life. Because he chose to do so.

www.ingramcontent.com/pod-product-compliance
Ingram Content Group UK Ltd.
Pitfield, Milton Keynes, MK11 3LW, UK
UKHW062002290726
14090UKWH00021B/1343